THE NE[...]
NIPPY G[...]
CANTER[...]BY

*Victorian eyebrows – and blood pressures –
were raised when this bare-breasted beauty
representing the Muse of lyric poetry,
was revealed when the Marlowe
memorial was unveiled in 1891.*

Alan Major

By the same author
A New Dictionary of Kent Dialect. Meresborough Books
Whose Buried Where in Kent. Meresborough Books
Hidden Kent. Countryside Books
Cherries in the Rise. S. B. Publications
Goldings, Napoleons and Romneys. S. B. Publications
A Kentish Childhood. S. B. Publications
Kentish As She Wus Spoke. S. B Publications
A Little Book of Kent. S. B. Publications

First published in 2004 by S. B. Publications,
19 Grove Road, Seaford, East Sussex BN25 1TP

ISBN 1 85770 296 4

Cover design by EH Graphics. Tel: 01273 515527
Designed and typeset by CGB, Lewes. Tel: 01273 476622
Printed by Ethos Productions Ltd.

INTRODUCTION

This book has two purposes. It is for people with limited time available who want to see as much as they can in the hours they have in the city in which I have lived for more than thirty years.

The second purpose is to tell the reader about some of the curious and surprising things there are to see in Canterbury. It is so annoying to read about something of unusual interest later and realise – 'We walked right past that and didn't know it was there'. With this book to hand that situation can be avoided.

The area covered is restricted to Canterbury within the city walls, excepting St. Dunstan's Street which is included as a starting place because it was – and still is – the main approach to the city. However, the book is so arranged that the reader can dip into it and select a specific item or area to explore. Perhaps memorials of past wars, of which Canterbury has many – or old churches still standing after centuries but today used for secular purposes.

The thoroughfares that lead to the cathedral, the chief aim of visitors, are all connected and within walking distance of each other. So, with the aid of the eight not-to-scale sketch maps that show what is where in each section of the city – **PC** indicates a public convenience, **PO** post office – no problems should occur.

ALAN MAJOR
CANTERBURY
2004

The St Dunstan's Street approach to Canterbury, photographed from the battlements of the Westgate. A safety-conscious city council has placed a shatterproof screen round the waist-high parapet – hence the shaded area and line across the sky in this picture.

ST DUNSTAN'S STREET

Starting on foot from the church we can follow the same route as that taken by King Henry II on 18 July, 1174 – but with our shoes on. He arrived on horseback with his entourage at the church, changed from his royal finery into the sackcloth garment of a penitent and walked barefoot to the Westgate.

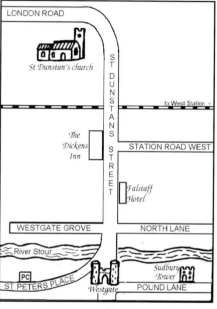

A crowd lined the route as word had got round that the king was doing penance for having lost his temper with Thomas Becket and brought about the archbishop's murder by asking, in exasperation: 'Will nobody rid me of this turbulent priest?'

Four knights, keen to curry royal favour, did just what the king asked. They rode from Saltwood Castle to Canterbury on 29 December 1170 and slew the archbishop in his own cathedral, slicing off the top of his head and depositing his blood and brains on the stone floor of the northwest transept – a spot now known as the Martyrdom.

This dastardly deed shocked all Christendom and the blame for it was placed squarely upon the king. In an attempt to restore his reputation Henry made this penitential progress through an earlier Westgate – the present one was built in 1380 – along St Peter's Street and into Mercery Lane. When he reached the cathedral he was escorted to the crypt and stripped of his sackcloth garment.

The naked king then bent forward over Becket's tomb, poured forth his contrition for the hasty remark that had resulted in such dire consequences, and prepared to be publicly scourged by the assembled ecclesiastics. The bishops and abbots each administered five strokes of the rod and the monks three. Henry then spent a painful night kneeling by the tomb in silent prayer and next day he left Canterbury, formally cleansed of his 'crime'. The knights, who had taken their king's rhetorical question so seriously and slain the archbishop, lived out their lives unpunished.

St Dunstan's church is open every day. Inside is the Roper family vault in which lies the head of Sir Thomas More, Lord Chancellor of England and author of that sixteenth century best-seller, *Utopia,* which describes the idyllic socialist state in which all possessions are held in common and education is freely available to both men and women. He was beheaded for refusing to accept Henry VIII's assumption of authority over the English Church.

His daughter, Margaret, wife of William Roper, MP for Canterbury, bought her father's head from his executioner and had it placed in a niche in a wall of the vault. This account of an event that took place in 1535 was confirmed in 1978 when the vault was re-opened on the 500th anniversary of Sir Thomas More's birth and a human skull was found there.

6

Closer to the Westgate, at 71 St Dunstan's Street, is what is now known as 'the Dickens Inn at the House of Agnes'. The House of Agnes was, according to a Canterbury resident who was a friend of Charles Dickens, the one the famous author had in mind when, in *David Copperfield,* he described the house Agnes Wickfield lived in as:

> . . . a very old house bulging out over the road, a house with low lattice windows bulging out still further, so that I fancied the whole house was leaning forward, trying to see who was passing on the narrow pavement below.

There are, however, several other houses in the city that lay claim to this Dickens connection.

Opposite the inn is the road leading to Canterbury's West Station by the pillared entrance of which is a plaque stating that the world's first railway season tickets were issued from there in 1834. The plaque also records that:

> 'NEAR HERE WAS THE TERMINUS OF THE CANTERBURY & WHITSTABLE RAILWAY, 1830 (GEORGE STEPHENSON, ENGINEER).

Inns and hostelries were established in St Dunstan's Street to offer rest and refreshment to travellers who arrived late, found the Westgate shut, and had to spend the night outside the city walls. One such was what is now the Falstaff Hotel at 8 to 10 St Dunstan's Street. From the wrought-iron bracket that still projects over the pavement hung a large sign depicting a jovial, Falstaffian figure. It has since been replaced with the smaller one, pictured above, which shows a bare-legged old man drinking from a bottle.

POUND LANE

There is an extensive length of the city wall in Pound Lane and only a few yards along it from the Westgate are two bastion towers that have

Sudbury's Tower.

been converted into private houses. Neither are open to the public but can be seen from the lane. One of them, Sudbury's Tower, is said to be haunted by the ghost of Simon of Sudbury who, when Archbishop of Canterbury, paid to have the Westgate built. However, the tall, grey-bearded and grey-cloaked ghost who always politely knocks on the door before entering a room, differs from Simon in one important detail. He is not headless.

Simon of Sudbury's ghost would have been – for the archbishop was dragged from the Tower of London, where he had taken refuge with other officers of state,

and had his head chopped off by Wat Tyler's rebels in the Peasants' Revolt of 1381.

THE WESTGATE

Looking at the sheer size of the Westgate it is difficult to believe that it would be logical for a circus proprietor to ask the city council if he could pull it down because it was too low and narrow for his elephants. But that, according to a story that circulated in the city in the early 1900s, is what a Mr Wombwell did in 1850. His proposal was discussed at length by the city council and, when put to the vote, the result was a tie. It was only the mayor's casting vote that saved the Westgate.

This story has been re-told and believed over the years. But it was all a figment of the imagination of Francis Bennett-Goldney, who in 1905 served Canterbury as its mayor and, from 1910 until his death in 1918, as its Member of Parliament.

Francis was born in Birmingham and changed his surname from Evans to his mother's maiden name of Bennett-Goldney, so he said, in order to inherit the family fortune. The story of Wombwell and his menagerie was a fictional 'fact' contained in Bennett-Goldney's book, *The History of the Westgate* to hot up a dull history

It is surprising that this tall tale has been accepted, even to the present day, for double-decker buses and heavy goods

The Westgate, from North Lane.

vehicles much larger than elephants manage to edge through the stone archway of this medieval gateway although, admittedly, some do scrape the sides and damage their paintwork.

And why go into the city with the menagerie anyway, except perhaps as a publicity parade? On Canterbury's northern outskirts is Kingsmead, listed as King's Meadow in the Domesday survey of 1086. This open space near the river was where travelling fairs and

circuses camped and gave performances. Which is why the design of the large supermarket now on the site is a representation of a half-erected 'big top'.

Earlier in its history there was a real threat to the Westgate. The increasing numbers of stagecoaches and farm wagons bringing people and produce into the city were causing the equivalent of modern traffic jams. Narrow Eastbridge in central Canterbury was a particularly bad bottleneck.

To remedy the situation the city's Commissioners of Paving, Lighting and Watching issued an order in 1787 requiring a number of thoroughfares to be widened and nothing was to project more than twelve inches onto, or over, a pavement, road or street. This resulted in the demolition of all the city's gates, except the Westgate which was retained because it served as one of the city gaols and there was always plenty of demand for its accommodation.

The Westgate from St Peter's Street. The entrance to the museum is under the central archway.

Debtors and other hard-luck prisoners were kept in an iron cage on the ground floor so they could beg for food and alms from passers-by. More violent criminals were upstairs in the cells, chained by their hands and feet to the walls.

The Westgate, with its twin drum towers, was built about 1380 of Kentish ragstone, each block being shaped by hand. When the curfew bell sounded at 9pm all the gates were closed and nobody could enter or leave the city.

Travellers who arrived later and found the Westgate's drawbridge up and its portcullis down might hopefully shout their name and business to the guards and ask nicely: 'Can we come in please?' But unless the person was of high rank and had been expected but delayed, no one would be admitted.

For those in the condemned cell there was only one way out. They were paraded through the city's main streets, sometimes 'assisting' by carrying the timber to build the gallows on which they would be hanged – either on Oaten Hill or on Wincheap Green. After 1780 prisoners were taken straight from the condemned cell and hanged beside the Westgate, thus being spared the walk to their death carrying the means for it.

The museum inside the Westgate displays a collection of armour and weapons and relics from the First and Second World War and the building's grim history is reflected by a quantity of cuffs, chains, screws and other restricting devices. In the floor above the arch are some large 'murder holes' through which the city's defenders poured boiling animal fat and dropped heavy objects on the heads of any invaders. These holes are now covered with strengthened glass and visitors can look down – but not drop anything – on the traffic passing below.

In a cell in the southwest corner of the battlements, overlooking Westgate Gardens, is a waxen effigy of a sixteen year-old boy. He was kept

The 'prisoner in the tower'.

there in solitary confinement because, reported the *Kentish Gazette* in 1793, he was so incredibly strong that he could break all the usual cuffs and chains used to restrain the other prisoners.

THE WESTGATE GARDENS

We are now within the city walls. Ahead is the pedestrianised St Peter's Street and to the right is St Peter's Place, a busy through road

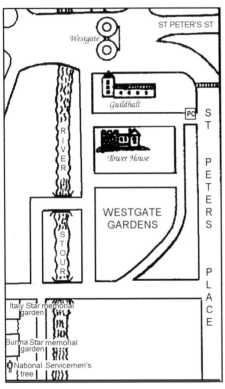

of Regency-style terraced houses. A conveniently placed pedestrian crossing gets us to the former Holy Cross church in which, since it was made redundant, Canterbury City Council has held its meetings. The original city Guildhall in Guildhall Street was badly bomb-damaged during the war and was demolished.

Past this seat of local government is the riverside path entrance to the Westgate Gardens or, if we turn left before reaching the Guildhall, we are on another access path to the gardens that takes us past a fourteenth century flint bastion, originally part of the city wall. Adjoining it is the seventeenth century Tower House in which the Williamson family lived for fifty years before giving it, in 1936, to the city council together with the land occupied by the gardens. It has, since then, been used as the Mayor's Parlour where visiting dignitaries are received and entertained.

The gardens by the riverside, the Tower House and the former Holy Cross church viewed from the Westgate's battlements.

Short lengths of the city wall are missing in this area because in 1647 the then mayor, a staunch Puritan, decreed that there was to be no holiday jollity on Christmas Day. All the shops were to be kept open and a market held as usual. However the citizens thought otherwise. They seized the mayor, set prisoners free from the gaols, smashed up the market stalls, secured plenty of free ale and played a kind of football in the streets. Armed Trained Bands were sent to restore order and they had to burn down the wooden doors of the Westgate to get in to the city. To avoid being shut out again they blew holes in the wall near the castle and pulled down parts of it near the Westgate.

The Tower House, now the Mayor's Parlour, beside city wall bastion.

The gardens contain an unusual memorial in the form of an Arbutus tree, planted in 2000 by the city council to commemorate the hundreds of

National Servicemen from Kent – the author was one of them – who served the country in war and peace between 1947 and 1963. The tree stands on the west bank of the river beside the Italy Star and Burma Star memorial gardens.

ST PETER'S STREET

This is the longest, straightest street in central Canterbury. It is named after St Peter's church, pictured left, which is set back from the road and behind its railing-topped wall and iron entrance gate has a garden filled in summer with roses, hollyhocks and other cottage garden flowers. It also has a fine Norman tower and a gem of a Bethersden marble font.

On the same side as the church is 23 St Peter's Street, the birthplace of Thomas Sidney Cooper, painter of cattle, sheep and local pastoral scenes.

Unlike others who found fame and fortune Cooper did not desert his native heath but lived on the outskirts of the city at Harbledown until his death in 1902 at the age of ninety-eight.

Cooper was a

generous benefactor. Not only did he give the city a number of his paintings but also set up a fund to provide coal and other necessities for its poor. When his mother, Sarah, died he bought and restored 23 St Peter's Street in her memory and opened it as an art school. One of the students of the Sidney Cooper Gallery of Art was Mary Tourtel, the creator of Rupert Bear, who studied there from 1891 to 1896.

When the school closed the premises were used as a community hall and called the Chaucer Centre. In the 1980s it became the Sidney Cooper Centre, a name by which it is still known by older residents although it was taken over by Canterbury's Christ Church University College in 2000, refurbished and opened as the Sidney Cooper Gallery,

Cooper bought his Harbledown house, Vernon Holme – named after his patron, Robert Vernon – by selling a

The Sidney Cooper Gallery.

painting entitled *Catching Wild Goats on Moel Siabad, North Wales* to George Furley, a Canterbury banker, for £1000 in 1863. This large picture is now in Canterbury's Royal Museum in the High Street. On the stairs is a portrait of Cooper by Walter W Ouless. The artist is shown seated, holding a palette and looking rather impatient, as if waiting for the viewer to arrive on time for a sitting.

THE FRIARS

On entering The Friars the first building to meet the eye is the Art Deco outline of the Marlowe Theatre which was built in 1933 as a cinema by the Odeon Company. So that it would not be confused with the Odeon Hall, then in St Peter's Street, it was named The Friars Cinema. There was another Marlowe Theatre, opened in 1951

15

in St Margaret's Street. It was also once a cinema – the Central Picture Theatre. The 1951 Marlowe Theatre was demolished in 1982 and the site is now occupied by part of the Marlowe Shopping Arcade.

In the forecourt of the present theatre stands a memorial to Canterbury's famous son, poet and playwright Christopher Marlowe who was born there in 1564. It is in the form of a statue called *Lyric Muse,* created by E Onslow Ford. The lovely lady with her lyre, pictured on the title page, has been shunted to several different sites since she was unveiled in the Buttermarket by Sir Henry Irving in 1891. Her half-robed presence opposite the Christ Church Gate entrance to the Cathedral Precincts offended many Victorians but there she stayed until 1921 when she was moved to the Dane John Gardens. In 1993 the much-travelled statue arrived at its present site and was formally re-dedicated by actor Sir Ian McKellen.

A few yards past the car showroom adjoining the theatre is a bridge over the Stour from which, if we look down-river, we can see the two remaining medieval buildings of the Dominicans, or Black Friars. They came to Canterbury in 1237 and built their house over and by the river a decade or two later. It had a refectory, a guest hall, an aisle-less church and confining cloisters. After the Dissolution of the Monasteries in 1538 the buildings were used for a time as a weaving

hall by Protestant Walloon weavers who had fled from the Low Countries to escape religious persecution by the Spanish.

In the seventeenth century the Baptists moved in to the refectory and Daniel

The Blackfriars refectory, on the east bank of the Stour looking up-river.

Defoe, author of *Robinson Crusoe,* preached to them there. Today the refectory is the King's School art centre and the guest hall a community centre.

On the left bank, looking up-river from the opposite side of the Friars bridge, is a low, chapel-like brick building with a tower at one end of it where, so legend says, a medieval alchemist tried to turn base metal into gold.

There might have been earlier buildings on the site to give rise to this tale for the present 'tower' certainly looks more mid-Victorian than medieval. Perhaps it was originally a pinnacle obtained from another property in Canterbury and added as an ornament.

The alchemist's tower and opposite it a replica ducking stool.

From behind The Weavers, on the opposite bank, a replica ducking stool projects out over the river, ready to immerse any female scold or scandalmonger in the chill waters of the Stour. Canterbury had a ducking stool which was in use until the end of the eighteenth century.

It also had another politically incorrect way of dealing with women who talked out of turn. In the Museum of Canterbury is a scold's bridle – an iron frame that fitted over the head, with an iron plate at the front which was placed in the miscreant's mouth and clamped down over her tongue.

If we retrace our steps from the Friars we are back at the eastern

end of St Peter's Street and on the way to possibly the second most photographed building in Canterbury. It is The Weavers – a row of much-restored timber-framed tenements built about 1500, with a frontage to St Peter's Street and running along the riverside at King's Bridge.

The Weavers, pictured left, was used by, and named after, the Flemish weavers who arrived in the city in the 1540s and congregated by the river because its water was necessary for the prod-uction of various types of cloth. They were followed by the Walloon silk weavers from the Low Countries and these French-speaking Protestants were given a chapel in the crypt of the cathedral in which to worship. Canterbury was at that time a centre of the wool and cloth trades and these early asylum seekers were welcomed, the city council promising freedom to live and work for any who wanted to 'set up, use and exercise the feat and mystery of making, weaving or sowing of cloth.'

In 1676 there were about 2,500 'foreign' weavers in Canterbury in 125 businesses run by master weavers who employed some 700 English assistants, but by the end of the eighteenth century the wool weavers had moved up north and silk weaving had ceased as a result of the competition from cheaper imports from the East.

On the other side of the street, and partially built over the Stour, is Eastbridge Hospital. It was set up in the twelfth century by Edward Fitzodbold as the Hospice of St Thomas upon Eastbridge and was later on combined with the Hospital of St Nicholas and St Katherine that had been established next door by a wealthy merchant to care for 'poor pilgrims, infirm persons, the destitute and homeless and lying-in women'.

Eastbridge Hospital.

Healthy but poor pilgrims were allowed to stay one night for bed and breakfast at a cost of fourpence. Ailing pilgrims, even pregnant women, could stay until healthy or had become mothers. Should any of them die before they got to St Thomas Becket's Shrine they were given a permanent resting place close to it – beneath a now turf-covered graveyard in the Cathedral Precincts.

After the destruction of the shrine in 1538 the numbers of pilgrims declined and the hospital was first converted into a school for children of poor families and then became an almshouse. Today it still provides accommodation for the elderly and its undercroft, refectory and two chapels have been restored and are open to visitors. The chapel at the top of the stairs that lead to the upper floor has a late twelfth or early thirteenth century painting in tempora of *Christ in Majesty*, possibly by artists of the Canterbury Cathedral School of Painters. The larger chapel, reached up another short flight of stairs, has a much clearer, more detailed *Christ in Majesty.* Do take a look at the complicated woodwork used to support the weight of the thirteenth century roof of this chapel. It is a rare type known as king-strut and scissor braced, with a light-allowing spirelet.

Beyond King's Bridge is the High Street and on the right, above the entrance to the post office is an ornate trade sign. It was put up in 1866 when the premises were the offices of the Invicta Fire Insurance Company. It also records, with its hand axes and hose branches, the founding of Kent Fire Brigade in 1821. The sign, which has recently been restored, was made by John Blashfield, a craftsman in this art who exhibited at the Great Exhibition, 1851.

BEST LANE

Numerous streets, roads and lanes in Canterbury are named after saints. This is the only one, as far as I have been able to trace, that is named after an innkeeper. In 1660 Charles II arrived in Canterbury from Europe on his way to London to be restored as king and was, it is said, lavishly entertained at a former Three Tuns by mine host whose surname was Best. To commemorate the royal visit to the inn in this lane it was known afterwards as Best's Lane which has since been shortened to Best Lane.

STOUR STREET

On the right-hand side, almost opposite Jewry Lane, is the arched entrance to the house of the Grey Friars. Nine grey-habited members of the Order of Francis of Assissi arrived from Normandy in September, 1224 and for two days were guests of the Cathedral Priory monks. Four moved on to London but five decided to stay in

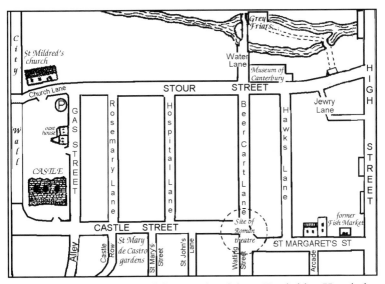

Canterbury and began to minister to the sick at Eastbridge Hospital.

They lived in wattle and daub huts in the garden of the Poor Priests' Hospital until 1267 when Sir John Digge, obtained land for them by the river on which they built the first Franciscan friary in England.

Only the two-storey flint, stone and brick building, pictured right, survived the destructive force of the Dissolution. Today services are held on Wednesdays throughout the year in the chapel upstairs and visitors are welcome. The rest of the building can be viewed on weekday afternoons from Easter to September.

One of the ground floor rooms was used as an overflow gaol in the nineteenth century and on its wood-panelling is some still readable graffiti of the 'KILROY WAS HERE' type. 'T WOOLLETT' noted that he was there for 'fourteen days for rum-running' in 1819 and T PIDDOCK was in residence on 'APREL 17' of the same year,

The Poor Priests' Hospital, now the Museum of Canterbury.

The Poor Priests' Hospital began in 1175 as the home of a mint master who had to leave the area quickly five years later possibly to avoid having his right hand amputated – the usual punishment for issuing debased coinage.

In the sixteenth century its use as a hospital for ailing and infirm priests ended and it became the property of the city authorities. For a time it was the Bluecoat School for boys, then a poor house, a gaol, a furniture store, an organ-building workshop, a St John's Ambulance headquarters, the East Kent Regiment's museum and the council's health department and clinic.

Invicta in wartime, surrounded by the concrete 'dragon's teeth' of an anti-tank blockade. Photo: Tony Blake

Now it is the Museum of Canterbury and visitors are taken on a time-walk through the city from the first century AD to the present day.

Stephenson's *Invicta*, the steam locomotive used on the Canterbury-Whitstable line, is safe and dry indoors after years behind railings near the Riding Gate and

Mary Tourtel's creation, Rupert Bear has a museum of his own as part of the complex.

Turn right at the museum's entrance gate and continue along Stour Street to the tree-lined Church Lane and the eighth century Church of St Mildred, the oldest

St Mildred's church with its chapel chimney but without its tower.

church within the city walls. Its south and west walls are partly Saxon and contain some Roman tiles, added, no doubt, from ruins in the area by the re-builders after a fire in 1246. The church acquired an unusual feature – a fireplace – when a family chapel was added to the south-east side of the chancel in the sixteenth century but it has lost its tower. It was demolished in 1832 and all the stone, flint and wood of which it was built was sold, as were the bells.

GAS STREET

There cannot be many, if any, towns in which a Norman castle shared its site with a gasworks. Canterbury is, or rather was one, for the gasworks have gone, their foundations buried beneath the car park and the houses that line one side of this paved street.

The wooden motte and bailey castle built in 1066 on an earlier Roman mound further to the east was replaced in the reign of Henry I by a three storey, almost square, keep with flint and stone walls 80 ft high and 14ft thick. It was built to control a section of the London to Dover Road but it hardly saw any serious action. In 1216 the castle surrendered to the Dauphin, Louis of France, who hurried over to help sort out the argument between the barons and King John. It was also meekly handed over to Wat Tyler and his rebels in 1381.

They freed the prisoners from the three-windowed basement used as a gaol, did some looting, then set off for London to kill Archbishop Simon Sudbury.

Canterbury Castle, without its top storey.

It was decided to demolish the castle for its stone in 1817 and the top floor was taken off. However, the job proved too tough and too costly and was abandoned. In 1825 the Canterbury Gas Light, Water & Coke Company took it over and removed all the internal walls to create a store for coal and coke for the neighbouring gasworks. Machinery was also installed to pump river water into a large cast-iron tank – as a fire precaution, no doubt.

A century or so later the city council bought the castle keep from the gas company. Today it is open to visitors and they have a choice of entrances – from Church Lane; through an iron gate by the former oast house in Gas Street; and from Castle Street which we have now reached.

CASTLE STREET

On the right-hand side, between Castle Row and St Mary's Street, are the St Mary de Castro Gardens This used to be the poor quarter of Canterbury and in 1486, because the parish of St Mary de Castro could no longer afford to maintain its church, it was amalgamated with St Mildred's and the small congregation of the former moved to the latter. St Mary's crumbled into ruin but its churchyard continued to be used as a burial ground until it was full. Adjoining this graveyard-now-gardens is the White Hart inn.

It was formerly the mortuary and sheets that covered the corpses are still in its cellars.

Further along Castle Street, at the junction of Watling Street, Beer Cart Lane and St Margaret's Street, is the present Three Tuns inn, on the side of which is a large notice stating that:

THIS INN LIES ON THE SITE OF CANTERBURY'S ROMAN THEATRE, FIRST BUILT ABOUT THE SAME TIME AS THE COLISEUM IN ROME

It gives further information to the effect that the theatre was rebuilt about 210 AD 'as one of the largest theatres in Roman Britain' and although its walls were 'robbed out' by the twelfth century 'much remains beneath the ground'. And indeed it does. Excavations have revealed a huge D-shaped structure with 12ft thick outer walls and a diameter of 232ft. There is also evidence that, as the notice states, there was an earlier and larger 320ft diameter Roman amphitheatre on the site.

Watling Street retains the name it had as a Roman road although it was abandoned as a main thoroughfare in Canterbury about 900 AD as a result of the river changing course and the water level rising.

Number 16 Watling Street is believed to be the earliest surviving brick-built town house inside the city boundary. It was modernised in the eighteenth century but of necessity its garderobe (lavatory) was kept and it projects from the side of the end wall of the property. When seen from the street it is an outside loo, but it is also an inside one – if you see what I mean.

ST MARGARET'S STREET

On the west side of this short street is the church after which it was named – St Margaret's. It was declared redundant some years ago and now houses *The Canterbury Tales* visitor attraction. This is a reconstruction in tableaux, sound and with the occasional smell, of how fourteenth century Canterbury's streets looked and were populated – with shops, tradesmen, even a streetside dentist – also the journey made by Geoffrey Chaucer and his band of pilgrims from the Tabard Inn at Southwark to the Shrine of St Thomas. On the way to Canterbury the Knight, the Miller, the Nun's Priest, the Pardoner and the much-married Wife of Bath tell their *Tales* and visitors are asked before they leave to vote for the one they liked best. The attraction is open throughout the year, except on Christmas Day, and is well worth the admission charge if only to find out, from the Wife of Bath, what it is that every woman desires.

Opposite the church stood the Fountain, the second oldest inn in England – until 1 June 1942 when it was destroyed in an air raid. Now on the site is the modern Marlowe Arcade with its shops under cover.

A few steps away, on the other, west side of the street, is Canterbury's former Fish Market. It is hard to believe that behind the classical Grecian frontage, pictured left, there were once marble slabs heaped with dogfish and soles from Dover, Medway flounders, Ramsgate herrings, Deal crabs, Gravesend and Pegwell Bay shrimps, Whitstable whelks and oysters. For a time some of the pillars were hidden by a false shop front but this was removed when a scheme to bring Canterbury's shop fronts back to how they were originally was introduced. Next door there is a fish and chip shop . . .

A Sidney Cooper lithograph of the High Street in 1827.

HIGH STREET

On the High Street side of the Stour Street/Best Lane junction there is another of the city's famous buildings. The elaborate cartouche on the centre gable declares it is:

THE BEANEY INSTITUTE, PUBLIC LIBRARY
AND MUSEUM

and a board above the entrance informs us that we are about to enter the:

ROYAL MUSEUM AND FREE LIBRARY
FOUNDED 1858.

The 'Beaney', as it is called by all who know it well, has an ornate frontage with stained glass and clear windows and pink tessellated and plain panels between decorative and plain

The 'Beaney'.

half-timbering. Which is an elaborate way of saying that it is pseudo-Tudor with a touch of ancient Roman and some Scottish baronial.

Enter by its glass doors and you are in the public library, reference library, local archives and recorded sound library. On the first floor, reached by the grandest of wooden staircases, is the museum of the East Kent Regiment, the 'Buffs'. In the gallery adjoining it is the city's picture collection with a room devoted to the life and works of Thomas Sidney Cooper with numerous examples of his paintings. To the left is the special exhibitions gallery and the museum's collection of pottery and porcelain from Greek and Roman times to the present day.

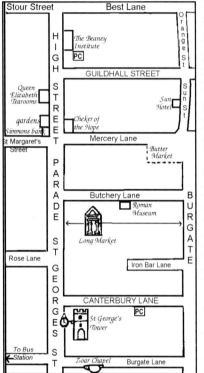

Why the 'Beaney'? Because James George Beaney, a Canterbury labourer's son who became a doctor, went to Australia in 1857 at the time of the gold rush and made a fortune. But it was not in the goldfields that 'Diamond Jimmy' as he was known to his friends, became rich.It was on the operating tables of Australia. His flashy lifestyle and success was criticised by rivals, for there were a high number of fatalities as a result of his surgery. He was tried once for murder and twice for manslaughter after unsuccessful operations, but survived them all professionally.

When he died he left £10,000 to build the Beaney Institute and public reading room 'for the education of the labouring man.' And to make doubly sure his name would be remembered in his native city he left £1,000 to the Dean and Chapter to place a memorial to him in the cathedral's nave. He left virtually nothing to his destitute sister.

On the opposite side of the High Street, a little way past Guildhall Street on the right, is Queen Elizabeth's Tea Rooms. These premises, with the plasterwork on their upper frontage picked out in pale blue and white on a soft pink background, date from 1573 and are on the site of the medieval Crown Inn. Certainly Good Queen Bess did stay at St Augustine's Abbey, on the east side and beyond the city wall, on her fortieth birthday, but there is no record of her

Queen Elizabeth's Tea Rooms.

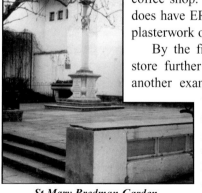

partaking of tea and cakes in what has since been named her tea rooms – and is now a coffee shop. However, a large upper room does have ER monograms in the decorative plasterwork on the ceiling.

By the front entrance of a department store further down the High Street is yet another example of a former churchyard which has been turned into a small off-street garden. This garden, according to a plaque on a wall, is on the site of St Mary Bredman, a Norman church that was rebuilt in 1828

St Mary Bredman Garden.

and demolished in 1900. As well as a horse trough inscribed:

TO OUR PATIENT COMRADES OF THE HORSE LINES

there is, in the centre of the garden, a memorial to the officers, NCOs and men of the Royal East Kent Yeomanry 'raised 1794, disbanded 1921', and the Kent Yeomanry.

MERCERY LANE

On the corner of the High Street and Mercery Lane is all that remains of the Cheker of the Hope, two thirds of which was

The Cheker of the Hope.

destroyed by fire in 1865. It was built towards the end of the fourteenth century as a pilgrims' inn by the Christ Church Priory at a cost of £867 14s 4d. It had several shops on the ground floor and round the yard at the rear was a gallery from which audiences could watch performances by bands of strolling players on a makeshift stage in the centre.

On the last lap of their journey to Becket's Shrine the pilgrims had to pass the gauntlet of vendors calling their wares from stalls in Mercery Lane, which was so-called because most of the shopkeepers there were mercers – the medieval English name for grocers. They would be exhorted to buy tin bottles of holy water, supposedly from Becket's Well in the cathedral crypt – but probably not. On sale, too, were badges cast in silver, lead or latten and bought by the pilgrims to prove to their family and friends back home that they had really made the journey to Canterbury.

Past and present architectural styles blend happily in Parade.

PARADE

The old and the new combine comfortably on the front elevations of this short parade of shops between the end of the High Street and the start of St George's Street. At street level they are nearly all twentieth century, with the upper storeys ranging from medieval to late Victorian.

There is no mistaking the age or the identity of a former occupant of No.3 for, at roof level, is a scalloped facade with its edges covered with a protective lead sheeting. Beneath a large central sunburst, are the words:

SUN FIRE OFFICE

and the date 1710 – which was the year this fire insurance company was started.

The name of 'Parade' comes from a former use. It was where the local militia drilled with their weapons.

BUTCHERY LANE

Originally it had a nicer name – Angel Lane – because at the end of it could be seen the cathedral's 235ft high steeple, called the Angel Steeple having on its lantern tower the figure of a golden angel representing St Michael, leader of the heavenly host.

Looking up Butchery Lane to the Bell Harry Tower.

This steeple was taken down in 1433 when work started on what became known as the Bell Harry Tower, named after a bell weighing 8cwt (400kg) called 'Bell Harry' after its donor, Prior Henry of Eastry. It is still rung each weekday for morning service and from 8.55-9pm for curfew, after which the gates of the Cathedral Precincts are closed for the night.

The tower, which was completed in 1504 with the addition of its four pinnacles, appears to be of stone but is actually built of brick – records varying, but up to 'a million and a half red bryks' – and faced with Caen stone.

Although wartime bombing destroyed some famous buildings it also exposed the foundations of others. In 1946 the remains of a Roman town house, c100 AD, were uncovered in Butchery Lane. One of its rooms had the floor paved with small blocks of stone like a mosaic, and with three patterned panels. Also in the house was a hypocaust, a device used by the Romans to provide underfloor central heating.

To see the house and other excavated items, go through the classical portico entrance in Butchery Lane and down a short flight of stairs to the new Roman Museum that runs beneath the shops of the Longmarket at the excavated level of *Durovernum*

Cantiacorum, the Roman Canterbury. There is no point in saying 'good morning' to the attendant sitting in his office operating a computer. He is no more real than the life-size and lifelike Roman cavalryman with his horse. But do look out for the large flat tile on which a Roman dog left its paw prints when he ran across it when the clay was wet.

The museum is open on weekdays throughout the year and on Sundays as well from June to October. It is closed Christmas Week and on Good Friday.

LONGMARKET

Why Longmarket? Because that is what was on the site originally – a long market. The Regency building had a ground floor hall full of traders' stalls and it stretched the entire length of Butchery Lane , parallel with it from St George's Street to Burgate. Its upper storey housed the Corn Exchange.

The Longmarket was damaged by fire during the war but the walls remained standing and it could have been restored. Instead it was

The pre-fabricated shops in 1953, decorated for the Coronation.
Photo: Tony Blake.

knocked down and a number of prefabricated shops built so that the

bombed-out traders could resume business. These prefabs were demolished in 1960 and replaced by what was intended to be a permanent shopping centre. However, the oblong box-style buildings that dominated the site were not popular with the public so down they came in the late 1990s and were replaced by modern medieval-style buildings with a paved piazza.

ST GEORGE'S STREET

Most of the properties in this street were destroyed in Second World War air raids – with a few exceptions. On one side is the original frontage of Marks and Spencer's department store. It was still standing after an air raid in 1942 and the store was re-built behind it. Further along is the tower of St George's, the church in which Christopher Marlowe was baptised in 1564.

The burnt-out shell of St George's church in 1952, its crenellations removed. Photo: Tony Blake

When the area was fire bombed in June, 1942, the church roof collapsed but the tower and the church's outer walls remained standing. After the war it was decided to straighten the street to make room for more shops – and remove the remains of the church in the process. The walls had been taken down and the crenellations stripped from the top of the tower when angry voices were raised in protest.The tower was speedily restored and its crenellations replaced.

The Victorian clock projecting from the tower was damaged and stopped when the church was bombed. The clock was removed, sent away to be repaired and on 6 May 1955 it was ceremonially unveiled on its frame supported by a crouching stone figure with a pained expression on its face. Which is not surprising as the frame and clock weigh 23cwt. There was one noticeable difference, however. The former

St George's tower today.

white dial with black numerals and hands was now a black dial with gilt numerals and hands.

AIR RAID STATISTICS

Some 445 high-explosive bombs and 10,000 incendiaries fell in the 135 air raids on the area, destroying 731 homes and 296 other properties. Numerous incendiaries fell on the cathedral roof but the fire-watchers either tipped them over the edge or extinguished them and threw them on to the turf below. A plaque with the names of these brave men and women was set in the cathedral's nave floor and unveiled in February, 2004. Many of the 115 civilian fatalities are buried in one area of the city cemetery in Westgate Court Avenue.

Off the south side of St George's Street is Whitefriars, named after yet another monastic order that moved to Canterbury in the fourteenth century. The White or Augustinian Friars, a contemplative order, settled in the parish of St George but not a stone of their buildings remain above ground. One of the White Friars, Brother John Stone, came to an extremely unpleasant end for refusing to accept Henry VIII as Head of the Church of England. In December 1539 he was dragged on a hurdle from the Westgate gaol and partially hanged on the Dane John Mound. Then, while he was still alive, his heart was removed and his limbs were cut off, boiled in oil, and affixed to some of the city gates to deter any like-minded clerics.

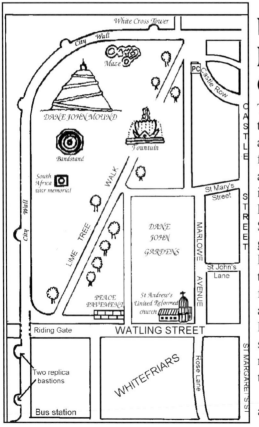

DANE JOHN GARDENS

These are longer than they are wide and, as can be seen from the map, there are a number of ways into them. At the Riding Gate-Watling Street entrance to the gardens there is the Peace Pavement on the left which features the work of artists from sixteen European cities that suffered bombing or major war damage in the twentieth century.

The names of the artists and the

numbers of the squares relating to each city are displayed on a plan of the pavement. Canterbury is No 7 and the artist is Barbara Ash. Visitors are invited to walk on the pavement and make their personal pledges for peace.

Another route into the gardens is past the modern shops in Rose Lane to Watling Street where, on the corner with Marlowe Avenue, is the bright new facade of St Andrew's United Reformed church. In 1939 Canterbury had two Congregational churches – the Countess of Huntingdon Connexion, which was destroyed by bombing in 1942 and an independent church. A new Congregational church was built on the corner of Rose Lane and Watling Street and became a United Reformed church when it joined doctrinally with St Andrew's Presbyterian church which was demolished in 1968.

St Andrew's United Reformed church.

The Rose Lane/Watling Street church was taken down in 2001 to make way for the Whitefriars shopping development on which work is currently in progress. It was replaced by the new St Andrew's church on the opposite, southern, side of Watling Street. It has a columned circular façade with a square 'tower' behind it to admit light into the interior. It also has an arched, grey dome – not quite on the scale of the Duomo in Florence or St Peter's in Rome, but nevertheless the first and so far the only dome on a church in Canterbury.

A third entrance to the Dane John Gardens is reached by crossing from Castle Street into an alley opposite the Keep. This leads to Castle Row from where there is access to the gardens and to the city wall.

Canterbury Council replaced a vanished rococo Victorian fountain with one in white Portland stone, sculpted by Joss Smith and has put up an exact replica of the bandstand that was demolished for its scrap metal in the 1939-45 war. It has also restored the South Africa war memorial which has an inscription on its south side carved by the artist-sculptor Eric Gill.

The fountain, the Lime Tree Walk and the South Africa war memorial.

To entertain the young visitors a wooden maze in the shape of a miniature castle and palisade was put up at the base of the Mound in 1999.

The Lime Tree Walk which crosses the gardens diagonally from north to south was created in 1790 by banker Alderman James Simmons. He had the area covered with turf, and a path provided a walkway, and lined it with lime trees at a cost of more than £1,500 – a considerable sum in those days. He also had the Dane John Mound raised to a height of 80ft high with a rather steep path leading to the top on which was placed, in 1803, a pillared obelisk of Portland Stone to his memory.

The Mound has been variously called Donjon, Dongeon, Dungil and Dungeon Hill but Dane John has become the accepted name for this first or second century Roman burial mound. There were two similar burials mounds in Canterbury. One that has been lowered and levelled is beyond the city wall and the ring road and its site is

' Dungeon Hill in Canterbury lately improved by the Liberality of Jas Simmons Esq' is the caption to this 1790 print.

occupied by a garage. The other was cleared when Canterbury East station was built.

According to a local legend the Dane John Mound was 'thrown up in a night' by the Danes to defend the city. This is unlikely as the Danish invaders usually visited Kent to raid, rape and pillage and did not stay long enough in one place to have need to defend it.

The flat, field-like area below and near the Mound was in the past used freely by Canterbury citizens as an open space as far back as the twelfth century. When the Black Death swept England in the winter of 1348 people suffering from it were housed in tents in the Dane John and those who died were buried in communal graves on the site. During the Civil War there was a gun emplacement on the Mound and when the 'brass gun' fired the reverberations

The Dane John Mound today with the castle maze at its base..

The Whitecross Tower with the Dane John Mound in the background.

broke the glass in many windows in Wincheap. One resident claimed and received compensation because the 'shooting of the gun did make his dwelling shake.'

From the entrance near Canterbury East station, in the area known as Worthgate close by the bridge crossing the ring road, the city wall runs in a north-easterly direction to link up with Burgate. Within a few yards of Worthgate is the first watchtower or bastion, known as the Whitecross Tower from the white stone cross which can be seen at its base from the ring road. It was placed there to commemorate the Protestants who were burnt at the stake for their faith in Martyrs Field, off Wincheap, during the Marian Persecution of 1554 to 1557.

This wall section of Canterbury's defences was built in the late third century AD and rebuilt in the fourteenth century on its Roman foundations. The five semi-circular, open-backed watchtowers each with three gun-loops, like upside down keyholes, are some of the earliest in defence works in England.

The watchtowers between Worthgate and Riding-gate would have had fighting platforms from which archers could rain down arrows on unwelcome visitors.There was also a water-filled moat in front of them to keep the aggressors at a distance.

If the visitor carries on along the wall from the Dane John Mound towards the bus station the Dane John Gardens come to an end at Riding-gate, with the Peace Pavement on the left at ground level. Watling Street passes under the modern Riding-gate bridge which was built in 1970. The original Riding-gate, demolished in 1782, was where the Roman road entered the city from Dover. Its name, in Old English, is 'the Red gate', perhaps a reference to the red Roman bricks used in its construction. Look over the bridge parapet on the Dane John Gardens side to see the site of the foundations of the Roman and medieval gates, excavated in 1986, marked out in bricks in the street below.

The city wall continues beyond Riding-gate parallel with the bus station. Not all of the bastions here are ancient originals. Between Riding-gate and St George's Gate and Burgate Lane the two facing Upper Bridge Street and the ring road, on the east side of the wall, were built in the 1950s.

The bastion on the left, looking towards the Riding-gate bridge, looks flintily medieval but was built in 1955.

In 1830 a commodity and livestock market was built below this length of the wall. The moat, by then dry, was filled in and levelled; two crumbling medieval D-shaped bastions were removed to make more room for the market; and some semi-circular chambers were cut into the city wall to provide the auctioneers with some office space. In 1955, when the market moved to another site on the outskirts of Canterbury, the city wall was returned to its original form and the two demolished bastions rebuilt down to the last detail, including the gun-loops. The city wall slopes down into the east end of St George's Street and continues alongside the shops and department stores of Burgate Lane to link up with Burgate.

BURGATE LANE

Archaeologists excavating this area in 1954 found that when the fourteenth century city wall was built the earlier Roman wall had virtually disappeared and the little that was left was covered with medieval buildings. To bridge this gap in the city's defences a new bastion and stretch of wall had been constructed.

In 1801 a cistern was housed in this bastion to store some of the city's water supply and in 1845 a building on the site, incorporating part of the bastion, became the Zoar Strict and Particular Baptist

The chapel in the city wall bastion.

chapel. It is still there and services are held there on Sundays with weekday preaching on Thursdays. This little chapel is also licensed for marriages.

BURGATE

The name means 'chief route into the city', which it was in the distant past. Today it is a secondary street, part of it pedestrianised and mostly lined with post-war properties for the 1942 air raids destroyed almost all its early buildings. There are some left, however, to give the visitor an idea of what Burgate was like several centuries ago.

A little along on the left is the timber-framed No. 67, now the Moat Tea Rooms. On each side of its bow windows, at head height, are support brackets in the form of two

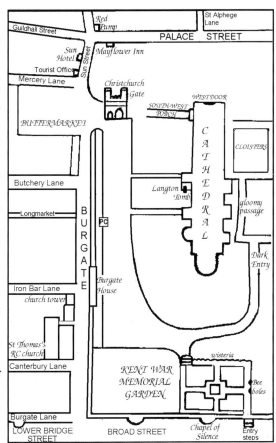

The pillared arcades and elegant neo-Georgian frontages of Burgate House.

grotesque carved wooden figures. Next door is the former Pilgrim's Shop, built in 1550.

When Canterbury was re-built after the war, many oblong and upright concrete and glass structures were put up with almost indecent haste and have since been taken down. However, those responsible for the redevelopment of the cathedral side of Burgate put up buildings in a traditional neo-Georgian architectural style, with the result that, further along, on the opposite side of the road, the post-war premises are most pleasing to the eye. Perhaps the most impressive is Burgate House which is built of brick with pillared arcades and an open pavement. The chimney-stacks are dummies added, presumably, for visual effect.

At one end, where the arcades run parallel with the roadway, there is an inscription in the brickwork, the lettering now hard to read, which states that:

In fact the Canadian Government paid for the greater part of the project which was the first post-war shopping development in Canterbury – and it is still standing

Almost opposite Burgate House is an early sixteenth century tower, all that remains of St Mary Magdalene church. It contains several monuments that were originally in the nave of the church which was not a victim of wartime bombing but was deliberately demolished.

The Reverend Richard Harris Barham, who wrote *The Ingoldsby Legends,* horror and burlesque tales in verse published in 1840 as a book, was baptised at St Mary Magdalene's in 1788. When his father died seven-year-old Richard inherited 61 Burgate, where he was born, and the manor house of

Tappington, on the Folkestone road near Denton, where later he did much of his writing. Before he was ordained in 1813 he founded the Wig Club in Canterbury – a society that met in a summerhouse in his Burgate garden to hold humorous debates about matters of the moment. The members, all young men of fashion, liked to wear preposterous wigs and parade about the city in lavish fancy dress.

Richard Barham, who was a Minor Canon of St Paul's in London, died in 1845. The large bronze plaque, pictured left, was unveiled on

No 61 after a memorial service at the city's Guildhall. The inscription on it gives quite a comprehensive account of the life of:

REV. RICHARD HARRIS BARHAM, B.A., AUTHOR OF THE INGOLDSBY LEGENDS, SON OF ALDERMAN BARHAM, MAYOR OF CANTERBURY, BORN HERE DECEMBER 6, 1788. A HUMORIST, A POET, A GENEALOGIST, AN ANTIQUARY, A CLERGYMAN, GREATLY BELOVED.
THIS TABLET WAS UNVEILED BY THE VERY REV. W.R. INGE, DEAN OF ST PAUL'S, 1930

Twelve years later 61 Burgate was destroyed by a bomb. The plaque was found among the ruins and is now on the front of the shop premises that have been built on the site.

Immediately adjoining the tower of St Mary Magdalene church, on its east side, is yet another grassed and paved off-street garden. Behind its low wall is the Roman Catholic Church of St Thomas of Canterbury in which there are two relics from the original shrine of St Thomas Becket – a finger bone and a piece of cloth. They can be seen in the Martyrs' Chapel of this Victorian Gothic church which opened for worship in 1875. Flanking the relics are statues of others who had the misfortune to get on the wrong side of a reigning

monarch – Thomas More, Chancellor of England; John Fisher, Bishop of Rochester and Brother John Stone, the Augustinian friar who was so brutally executed on Dane John Mound in 1539.

From the church continue west along Burgate past Iron Bar Lane, a name from the days when the city had livestock markets within its walls and certain streets were barred to stop cattle and sheep straying into, or out of them.

On the left past Longmarket is Butchery Lane and what was once a huge medieval inn, the White Bull. This building, pictured left, stretches all the way from the end of Butchery Lane to the Buttermarket. Not quite halfway down the lane can be seen, through an arched entrance, the original yard of the old inn.

BUTTERMARKET

Burgate ends at its junction with the cobbled, round, open area known as the Buttermarket. On one side, close to Mercery Lane's junction with the Buttermarket is Canterbury's tourist information office. On the north side, opposite Mercery Lane, is the Christ Church Gate entrance to the Cathedral Precincts.

This area is an American tourist's dream come true for it is easy to imagine Charles Dickens noting down details of a Victorian street scene from a bow window of the Cathedral Gate Hotel, one of the ancient and modern replica buildings now around the Buttermarket

The Buttermarket has not always been just that – a market selling butter. It was originally known as the Bullstake, because it was where bulls were tethered to be baited by dogs before being taken away for

The Buttermarket looking towards Burgate. The Christ Church Gate entrance to the Cathedral Precincts is on the left.

47

The Buttermarket in business in 1815 – the year of Waterloo.

slaughter. This was not done as a public sport. It was believed that treating the beasts in this way made the carcase meat more tender. However, it was the cruel sport of a public execution that brought crowds to the area in 1471 to watch a Mayor of Canterbury pay the penalty for an act of high treason against King Edward IV.

A building that served as an open air theatre was erected here in the early eighteenth century and replaced in 1790 with a large open-sided and circular structure with a roof supported on upright posts.

Was it ever a butter market? Yes, it was. Butter and similar commodities were traded there and records state that if the butter was not of a certain quality and weight the sheriff had the power, and used it, to confiscate the offending sample and fine the seller and supplier. The confiscated butter was not thrown away but sent to the Westgate gaol for consumption by the prisoners.

The Buttermarket's circular structure was taken down in 1888 as its roof was declared to be 'unsafe'. But it took several teams of horses quite a lot of time to drag the upright posts from the ground. In 1891, in its place, the *Lyric Muse* statue was unveiled by Sir Henry Irving as a memorial to Christopher Marlowe. The scantily clad beauty with her lyre was not considered suitable for the pious to behold on leaving the cathedral by the Christ Church Gate and she was replaced in 1921 by a memorial, pictured right, designed by Beresford Pite, to the men of the city killed in the First World War.

From the Buttermarket visitors to Canterbury have a choice. If time is short they can pay the admission fee at the Christ Church Gate, walk into the Precincts and visit the cathedral. If they have an hour to spare before doing so it can be well spent exploring the streets nearby.

SUN STREET

From the Buttermarket this street begins or ends, depending on which direction one is walking, at the shop on the west side of the Christ Church Gate. The original Sun Tavern, built in 1437, is now the fine, bow-windowed premises of a coffee shop and of the Cathedral Gate Hotel, on the east

side of the entrance to the Precincts. Both have interiors from the days when it was a tavern.

Did the street get its name from this tavern, as was the custom? Or from what is now 8 Sun Street, pictured left, a late medieval, three-storey property the upper storey of which has been restored with attractive red brick, herringbone infilling. This was, states a sign at first floor level, 'formerly the Sun Hotel, established in 1503. A shield-shaped plaque beside the sign has more information about this building. It was the Little Inn, made famous by Charles Dickens as the residence of Mr Wilkins Micawber, who offered that much-quoted advice about living within one's income to young *David Copperfield*.

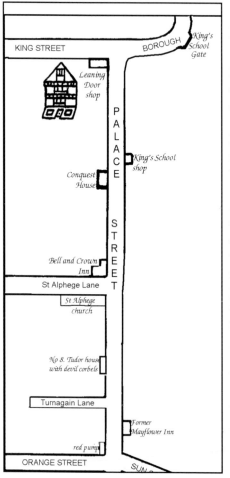

PALACE STREET

The Archbishop's Palace is only a short distance away – on the other side of the King's School wall which is halfway down on the east side – hence the name of this street.

Above the doorway of a shop on the corner of Orange Street is a replica of a small hand-operated water pump painted bright red. It seems a strange place to suspend such an object, especially as it has no connection with the goods sold in the shop.

But there is a genuine reason for it being there

As far back as 1703, there was, close to St Alphege church, a well from which water was drawn by a full-sized pump of this pattern. At an unspecified time this well was, for some unknown reason, filled in and the pump removed. In April 1870 when some roadworks were in progress, the 'Old Red Pump Well' as it was known in records, was re-discovered. It seems the original pump was placed on these premises as a trade sign until it rotted and was replaced by a smaller replica, pictured right. The pump was painted red to identify it as an emergency source of water to combat fires – a dangerous hazard in Canterbury's timbered properties.

Across from the replica pump, on the wall above the restaurant at No 59, is a painting of an early seventeenth century sailing ship on a rather rough sea and scrolls with the words: 'Traditionally the Mayflower Inn of the Pilgrim Fathers, 1601'. Today the ship is still sailing but the scrolls now advertise the restaurant and fully licensed Pilgrims' Bar in the premises below.

The link between the *Mayflowe*r in which the Pilgrim Fathers sailed to the New World, and this former Canterbury inn is Robert Cushman, a grocer's assistant who was married in St Alphege church in Palace Street. He had to flee to Leyden in Holland during the religious schisms that resulted from the Reformation for, among other 'sins', not attending church.

When things quietened down on the doctrinal front Cushman, by now a respected member of the Puritan community at Leyden, was authorised to return to Canterbury to see about obtaining a ship for the venture. A friend of his was James Chilton, a tailor in the city, and it seems reasonable to assume they met at the Mayflower Inn to make plans about emigrating.

The two carved figures on Tudor House, one of the HISTORIC HOUSES OF KENT *according to a diamond-shaped sign by the window.*

Numbers 8 and 17 Palace Street are two splendid sixteenth century half-timbered houses. On No. 8, known as the Tudor House or St Alphege's Priest's House, a few yards past Turnagain Lane, are two grotesque wooden figures on the brackets supporting the upper storey overhang. They are of indeterminate sex. The one on the right has his/her tongue out, the one on the left sports a handlebar moustache. Both are crouching forward, each squeezing very large female-type breasts between their hands.

The real purpose of these curious medieval corbels was to protect the property and the people in it from bad luck, illness and any other misfortunes which might otherwise befall them should they be visited by the Devil himself, whose imps they were. The figures were no doubt carved by the same craftsman who did the equally evil-looking ones on the Moat Tea Room in Burgate.

About halfway along on the west side of the street is St Alphege church. Its end walls and chancel windows abut on to Palace Street but the church porch entrance is round the corner in St Alphege Lane. In 1468 Thomas Prude gave as much money 'as would build a pillar' and it is there today with a brass stating:

GAUDE PRUDE THOMA PER QUEM FIT ISTA COLUMNA.

The church, yet another one to have become redundant, has been

*The Bell and Crown and next to it St Alphege church, and, below right, a
warning to those the inn considered as undesirable customers.*

put to good use. It is now the Canterbury
Environment Centre and it is open Wednesdays
to Saturdays from 10.30 am to 5pm.

On the other corner of St Alphege Lane, but
with its main entrance in Palace Street, is the red
brick and peg-tiled front of the Bell and Crown
inn. It was given this name in 1862 to
commemorate the marriage of Princess Alice,
Queen Victoria's second daughter, to Prince
Louis, Grand Duke of Hesse.

The earliest mention of a tenant of 'the corner
house opposite St Alphege' was in 1200 when it
was recorded that Peter Cook paid a quarterly
rent of '18 pence'. It was given to the cathedral
with other properties in 1225 and Walter
Bosewyne is named as the tenant in 1433. It did

TAKE
NOTICE
VAGABONDS,
DOG STEALERS,
HORSE THIEVES,
RAPSCALLIONS,
SCOUNDRELS,
LIARS
& ESPECIALLY
BURSARS!
WILL NOT
BE SERVED
ON THESE
PREMISES.

not become an inn until the seventeenth century and from then, according to the information board on the front wall:

The board also notes that the apty-named brewers, George Beer and Company, leased the inn in 1846 and the names of the innkeepers from 1862 to 2002 are listed on the left-hand side of the board and the Archbishops of Canterbury starting with Charles Longley in 1862 to Rowan Williams in 2003 on the right.

The Tudor frontage of No. 17, pictured left, now named Conquest House, conceals the building's medieval origins.

There, on 29 December 1170, so it is said, the four knights who had ridden from Saltwood Castle to Canterbury with the intention of gratifying King Henry II's wish to be rid of 'this turbulent priest' met in its undercroft to finalise their plans.

Then Reginald Fitz-Urse, William de Tracy, Richard Le Breton and Hugh de Morrville went on to murder Archbishop Thomas Becket in his own cathedral.

Canterbury's answer to the Leaning Tower of Pisa and, above, a closer look at the door.

Pisa has its famous Leaning Tower. Canterbury has its Leaning Door – at 28 Palace Street, a half-timbered, three-storey box-framed house that was formerly the King's School shop, and is now an art shop. What excites so much interest in these much-photographed premises is that the shop door and doorframe lean to the right at an alarming angle and the door has had to have pieces added to the top and sides to make it fit the frame. The ground floor frontage is also noticeably on the slant. But there is no need to fear that the whole structure is about to crash to the ground. It is only the timber frame that is leaning. Walk round the corner into the end of King Street and look at the building's side and rear walls and you will see they are supported by sound brickwork.

The distortion of the timber frame was almost certainly caused when, in the nineteenth century. a door was unwisely made through a ground floor inglenook and disastrously weakened the brick chimney breast, which was the building's main support. For about a century it listed and leaned, then one day the chimney that ran right through the house collapsed into the cellars.The premises were temporarily shored up and later on were skilfully restored to their present eye-catching appearance.

It is thought that this house, with its wealth of windows, was orginally the business premises of an Alderman Sabine. He had weavers – who would need good light – working on the upper floors and sold what they produced, and other goods, from his shop on the ground floor.

The next occupant was Sir John Boys, an Elizabethan lawyer, Member of Parliament, Canterbury's first Recorder and High Steward to the then Archbishop of Canterbury. In 1599 Sir John used his wealth to found Jesus Hospital as an almshouse for twenty people. It was in Sturry Road, which is outside the city walls, and one of the rules the inmates had to observe concerned the keeping of pets. Only cats, who were needed to deal with the rats and mice, were permitted on the premises.

Since Sir John Boys' day his house has had various uses. In the 1920s it was for a time called, not surprisingly, Ye Olde Curiositie Tea Shoppe.

THE BOROUGH

From the Leaning Door shop it is only a few minutes' walk into The Borough, a short curving street which links up with Northgate. On its east side is the Mint Yard entrance to the King's School with its flint and stone buildings set behind more high walls. Here there is another unusual door. On the left of the entrance there is a tiny wooden doorway within an archway, just large enough for King's School boys and girls to step through when the main gate is closed.

The entrance to Mint Yard leading to the King's School buildings. The small door is for the pupils to enter if the main gate is closed.

Mint Yard is so named because in the Middle Ages Archbishops of Canterbury had permission from the Crown to mint their own coinage within the cathedral precincts and this is where they did it.

In Mint Yard the visitor is surrounded by the buildings of King's School but there is a way along the paths of the grassed Green Court that leads to the rear of the cathedral. It passes through the shadowy, and infamous Dark Entry and bears right to the Cloisters. However, to enter the cathedral from its popular south-west entrance we must retrace our steps from The Borough along Palace Street, up Sun Street, again into the Buttermarket and to the Christ Church Gate.

CHRIST CHURCH GATE

This is the main entrance to the cathedral and is imposing and flamboyant in appearance. It was begun by Prior Goldstone II, who died in 1517, and was completed by Prior Thomas Goldwell in 1520. Its carved, panelled Caen stone has weathered over the years and has also been accidentally or deliberately damaged by man.

The Christ Church Gate in 1802, before its turrets were declared unsafe by the city surveyor.

The tall stone effigy of Christ which stood in the large central niche high up on the gate was used for target practice in 1642 by a group of Parliamentary soldiers supposedly under the command of the Colonel Edwin Sandys. They fired at least forty shots at it, aiming specifically at the statue's head and face which was badly damaged, and cheered when they hit it. Worse was to follow. In December, 1643, Parliamentary soldiers, aided by local Puritans, attached ropes to the statue, pulled on them and brought it crashing to the ground where it was smashed to pieces.. This was done as part of their intention to 'remove all items of superstition and idolatry' in churches and cathedrals.

Another version of the December 1643 destruction of the statue was that local people could not stand the sight of it any longer and removed it themselves without any help from Cromwell's New Model Army. The niche remained empty until 1991 when a sculptor, Klaus Ringwald, carved and gave to the Dean and Chapter the effigy of Christ that is filling it today.

It was also about 1643 that the original oak doors of the Late Perpendicular Gate were taken off their hooks and burnt by the Puritans. In 1660 some new oak doors were made and carved with the coat of arms of the Archbishop of Canterbury, William Juxon,

Archbishop Juxon's arms are on the main doors, and those of Dean Thomas Turner are on the smaller, oak postern door.

who, when Bishop of London had administered the sacrament to Charles I before his execution in 1649, and of his Dean, Thomas Turner. These doors are still in place.

Christ Church Gate was damaged deliberately in the early nineteenth century through the desire of banker James Simmons, of Dane John Mound fame, to see the cathedral clock from his bank at the corner of St Margaret's Street and High Street.

Simmons was founder and proprietor of the *Kentish Gazette,*

This ornate nineteenth century building is on the site of Simmons' bank.

twice served as mayor and was elected MP for Canterbury in 1806 so not surprisingly he had some local power and influence – and he liked to use it. Which is how, in 1803, Christ Church Gate lost its original two turrets.

One day, when Alderman Simmons was in conversation with city surveyor, Jesse White, in the foyer of the bank he was overheard by another customer to say : 'If those damn turrets of the cathedral gate were away we should see the clock from the bank's door. Can't you pull them down, Jesse?'

White's reply was reported to be: 'Certainly. It shall be done. No problem Alderman Simmons' – or words to that effect.

A little while afterwards the Dean and Chapter were informed by the city surveyor that the turrets were unsafe, too heavy for the gate and should be demolished. A month or so later they were gone.

The turrets were replaced in the 1930s when a member of the Friends of Canterbury Cathedral, Dame Janet Stancomb-Wills, gave £4,000 towards the restoration of the gate and her sister, Mrs Yda Richardson gave £3,200 for the turrets to be rebuilt..

The gate, with its new turrets was unveiled on 19 June 1937 by the founder of the Friends, Dr G K Bell, Bishop of Chichester, who had been Dean of Canterbury from 1924 to 1929.

Sadly neither of these two benefactors lived to see the restoration work completed, nor to see how their generosity has been a heraldic fashion.

On the left of the right upper window is a diamond-shaped lozenge bearing the coat of arms

Christ Church Gate today, from the Buttermarket.

of Dame Janet – on a field azure, three flying bees. Low on the left turret is another lozenge with the now barely-discernible lions' heads and anchors arms of Mrs Yda Richardson.

No serious damage was done to the gate and its doors by the wartime bombing, but over the years the weather has taken its toll on the row of stone angels and the shields they are holding and other heraldic shields and badges on the Buttermarket frontage.

THE CATHEDRAL PRECINCTS

After walking through the Christ Church Gate into the Precincts look back to its north face – it is so different and much plainer than the welcoming, much-ornamented south face. At the top is an angel holding a shield bearing the arms of Christ Church, Canterbury. Lower down is another angel bearing the arms of, possibly, Henry VIII, to the left of which is the rose-en-soleil badge of the Tudors and on the right a portcullis and another Tudor badge.

We now have a choice – either to go directly ahead through the southwest doorway entrance into the cathedral or walk around the Precincts.

To explore the Precincts bear right and continue eastwards until a narrow path on the left leading from the wider path is reached. This leads to the cathedral's southwest transept which adjoins the St Michael's or Warriors' Chapel.

Archbishop Langton's tomb jutting out from the east wall of the chapel

Now you would think an archbishop would be treated with respect when dead and buried. Particularly an Archbishop of Canterbury who was the leader of the barons who compelled King John to sign the Magna Carta, thus ensuring the continuance of the ancient liberties and laws of England.

When Archbishop Stephen Langton died in 1228 he was buried with all due ceremony in the apse of the Norman Chapel of St Michael. Then, 200 years later, along comes Margaret Holland and cuts his resting place virtually in half. She had the chapel altered in 1439 to accommodate her own tomb and that of her two husbands. In order that it should be in a central position the east wall of the chapel was arched over the mortal remains of Archbishop Langton, with the result that the feet end of his tomb projected out of the chapel into the open air, looking for all the world like a stone dog kennel.

Continue past the length of the cathedral and beyond it to a high-walled garden tended in medieval times by the monks. From 1682, the cathedral canons had a bowling green in this garden which was opened in 1921 to the memory of Kent's sons and daughters who died in the First World War.

The arched entrance from the Precincts into the garden.

The Kent County War Memorial Garden with the second oldest wisteria in the country on its west boundary wall.

The memorial, designed by Sir Herbert Baker, is in the form of a 27ft high Cross of Sacrifice on a stone column on which is carved a

crusader's sword, a ship and a wreath of roses and lilies. An oblong stone, pictured left, from the ruins of the Cloth Hall at Ypres in Belgium has been placed in the flint wall of a fifteen century bastion that has been roofed over and made into a Chapel of Silence.

Look carefully at the base of the wall on the north-east side of

the garden and you will see some curious holes, several feet apart, with angled bricks forming an arch above each of them.

The Chapel of Silence on the city wall.

No, they are not medieval cat flaps. They are medieval bee boles in which monks kept their skeps or straw hives for the bees from which they obtained honey and beeswax.

If we return to the Precincts through the arched entrance and follow a path to the right we pass the ruins of the priory infirmary and a cobbled path leads us into a covered passage and to the Dark Entry.

Here is Prior Selling's Gate of 1480

One of the bee boles in the base of the north-east boundary wall.

between Green Court, a large open quadrangle with, on the north side, the fourteenth century buildings of the King's School.

It was in this Dark Entry that the Reverend Richard. Barham, author of *The Ingoldsby Legends*, set a spine-chilling scene involving the ghost of the murdering maid, Nell Cook.

Turn left on entering the covered passage that leads past the Baptistery or Water Tower built in the twelfth century. Ahead is a gloomy passage, pictured below, that rivals the Dark Entry and at the end of it we

The Dark Entry looking towards the King's School Green Court.

come into the light of the Cloisters, on the ceilings and walls of which are many coats of arms and memorials to illustrious personages.   For a less formal and dignified but appealing human peep into the past look at the long stone bench that runs against the cathedral wall along the south side of the Cloisters. On it are fifty-six – yes, I have counted them carefully – incised footprints and handprints made by the boys of King's School. They produced the prints by pressing their shoes or their hands down onto

Three of the incised footprints, one of them dated 1714.

the stone seat and running a sharp pointed tool or knife around the edges to cut their outline into the stone. There are also incised initials and surnames – some of them of families still living in Kent – together with flags, outlines of churches, and other patterns.

In the eighteenth century the south wall area was a playground for the boys of King's School and belated restitution for any damage they might have done was made in part by a later generation. On 11 May, 1975, the pupils did a sponsored walk and raised money for the restoration of the bay in the Cloisters near to the stone bench with its incised graffiti.

From the Cloisters there is access to the north-east and north-west transepts of the cathedral. One is from the Dean's Steps near the Water Tower and another through the Martyrdom door. To reach the entrance used by the majority of visitors continue along the stone bench side of the Cloisters' covered walk, up some low steps into the open air and bear left to the west side of the cathedral.

The niches in the wall above and alongside the huge, but not usually open, west door, were occupied by carved stone figures of saints, popes and prelates up to the Reformation when, on orders from the Crown, they were all removed and destroyed. For some

300 years the niches remained empty. It is thanks to Dean Henry Alford and the sponsorship scheme he introduced in 1863 that they began to be filled again by the stone figures of kings, queens, princes, archbishops, ministers, politicians and other VIPs from the past that are there today.

The statues were supplied by a Belgian sculptor, Theodore Pfyffers, at a cost of £24 a figure and they were paid for by local church and lay dignitaries of the day. Records show that the Archbishop of Canterbury sponsored a statue of King Alfred. Dean Alford, who has his own niche on the north west tower, paid for Henry VIII and his wife for Queen Bertha. The 'Ladies of Canterbury' raised the required £24 for an effigy of the Black Prince.

Unfortunately Pfyffers used soft Caen stone for the figures. It is fine for use as building blocks but has not the durability of harder stone such as marble for three dimensional work. As a result the figures show much evidence of deterioration and fifteen have crumbled away since they were placed in their niches. No doubt

Dean Henry Alford, who started the buy-a-statue scheme, in his niche on the north-west tower.

Pfyffers used Caen stone in order to keep the cost down and he did try to prevent it eroding 'by silicating or imparting a hardened surface by a chemical solution of flint to each statue'.

The south-west porch of the cathedral, with statues of the great and the good in two tiers of niches.

There is a local legend to the effect that when all the niches are filled with statues the English monarchy will come to an end. Queen Victoria was presumably aware of this portent for when she was approached with a view to her statue and one of her Consort, Prince Albert, being placed there she asked how many niches would then be left empty.

She was told: 'Two, your Majesty', and she refused her permission. However, someone must have counted again for Victoria and Albert do occupy two of the niches and there are still twenty left vacant – surely enough to ensure the continuance of future generations of English monarchs for centuries to come.

Queen Victoria, who appears to have lost her sceptre to erosion, and Prince Albert on the west front of the cathedral.

The fifteenth century southwest porch and doorway, which is also ornamented with stone statues, is on the left past the west door. We have now reached the heart of Canterbury and, like the pilgrims before us, have fulfilled the ambition that stimulated the journey.

Now enter, examine and enjoy one of the finest cathedrals in the world. You will not be disappointed.

BIBLIOGRAPHY

Bateman, Audrey *The Magpie Tendency.* Privately published 1999

Blake, Philip H *Christ Church Gate, Canterbury Cathedral,* Phillimore and Company 1965

Crampton, Paul *Canterbury 1945-1975,* Tempus 2002

Crampton, Paul *Canterbury,* Chalford 1997

Gardner, Dorothy *Companion into Kent,* Methuen 1947

Hill, Rev Canon D Ingram *Canterbury Cathedral,* Bell and Hyman 1986

Lyle, Marjorie *Canterbury, 2000 Years of History,* Tempus 1994

Townsend, William *Canterbury,* Batsford 1950

Westwood, Kenneth J *Thomas Sidney Cooper of Canterbury,* Canterbury City Council Museums and Galleries Service 2003

Canterbury Churches Trail, Canterbury Environment Centre 2002

ACKNOWLEDGMENTS

The author acknowledges with thanks the assistance of the following in various ways during the preparation of this book:

DIANA M BAILEY, NEWICK.

TONY BLAKE, CHESTFIELD.

REV CANON M BUNCE, CATHOLIC CHURCH OF ST THOMAS OF CANTERBURY.

THE ORDNANCE SURVEY.

THE *KENTISH GAZETTE*.

He also wishes to thank his grand-daughter, Frances Buckworth for transferring his typed manuscript onto disk.

PICTURE CREDITS

The majority of the photographs are by the author. Those that are not are individually credited.

NOTES